Cele

...an observance for all believers in Messiah Yeshua, our Passover Lamb

James D Pace

©Copyright 2011
All rights reserved
Printed in the United States of America

No part of this book may be reproduced or transmitted in any form or by any means, electronic or mechanical, including photocopying and recording, or by an information storage and retrieval system, without permission in writing from the author.

ISBN 10: 1456593234
ISBN 13: 9781456593230

You may contact the Author at:
rabbij.d.pace@comcast.net

Table Setting

The Seder Plate

Z'roa Roasted Lamb Bone *in place of the Pesach (Passover) Lamb.*

Maror Bitter Herbs *(horseradish) used as a reminder of the bitterness of slavery.*

Karpas Green Vegetable *(parsley) symbolizes spring and rebirth, dipped in salt water representing tears*

Beitzah Roasted Egg *in place of the festival sacrifice (Chagigah-different from the Pesach sacrifice)*

Kharoset Mixture of Apples and Nuts. *Clay and mortar the Israelites were forced to make*

INTRODUCTION

Leader: We are glad you are here for this very special event. This evening we observe this meal in the same ancient tradition that it has been observed through thousands of years, since the first Passover. The Passover is the longest, continuing religious observance in world history. In a Jewish home, Passover is a special time of preparation, celebration and reflection because of the wonderful things that Adonai has done. As believers participating in this festival, we have a wonderful opportunity to acknowledge His mighty hand in our lives.

The Passover Seder tells the story of Adonai's mighty deliverance of the children of Israel from their bondage in Egypt. Rich in symbolism, this festival is a shadow of what was and is to come.

The Passover of today still points to Yeshua as the Messiah. Yeshua is the Hebrew word for Jesus, and is the name His mother gave him. Some other Hebrew words we will be using are "Adonai" in place of "God", "Seder" meaning "Order", as in order of service.

The next new word, "Haggadah", means "the telling" or "the story", and is the name given the book you will be following. It will be explaining the significance of practices, foods, and the blessings, we will be sharing. Unfortunately, it would take a week to cover in detail all of the symbolism of the Passover festival. Therefore, we give the leader the liberty to go into more or less detail at his discretion. There will be other words that we will explain as we come to them.

You will also need to select a Papa at your table. This person will be responsible for helping with the Seder plate and the Matzah. Instructions will be given throughout the Passover Seder as to his duties. Also, select a Mama at each table, to perform the traditional duties of lighting the Festival Candles.

Lastly this Haggadah contains many blessings transliterated from Hebrew; we will take time to help you with the correct pronunciations as we come to them.

SEARCH FOR THE LEAVEN

One of the instructions, during the preparation for Passover, is to remove all of the leaven from our homes. As it is written, *Seven days you shall eat unleavened bread, but on the first day you shall remove all leaven from your houses. (Ex 12:15)*

In our homes, the evening before the first day of Passover, the head of the household makes the final preparation by leading the entire family on a search for any remaining leaven in the home. It is customary to place a few small pieces of bread, throughout the home, so that some leaven is found.

The head of the household also takes with him, on the search, a feather, a candle and a piece of white paper. When the leaven is found, it is put in the paper and the feather is used to brush any remaining crumbs onto the paper. The paper is then rolled up, being careful not to spill, and the discovered leaven is disposed of by burning. A prayer and blessing are recited to acknowledge obedience to Adonai's Mitzvot (commandment), and to acknowledge that some leaven may not have been found, but asking that it be nul-and-void.

This is a great time for an object lesson for both adults and children. In Scripture, leaven, at times, is used to describe sin. We learn, through this tradition, how difficult it can be to get *all of the sin* out of our lives, and we ask forgiveness for our sins that we have discovered and those, at the time, we can't bring to mind.

LIGHTING THE FESTIVAL CANDLES

Leader: Our Seder begins with the lighting of two candles accompanied by a Blessing. As the light for the Festival of Redemption (Passover) is kindled by the hand of a woman, we remember that our Redeemer Yeshua, the Light of the World, came into the World as the promised seed of a woman. As we kindle the Festival lights, let us pray that the Spirit of Adonai will bring personal meaning to this Passover celebration.

(A woman from each table lights the candles)

Women: Baruch atah Adonai, Eloheinu Melech ha-olam, asher kidshanu b'mitzvo-tav, v'tzvanu, l'hadlik ner, shel yom tov.

All: Blessed are You, O Lord our God, Ruler of the universe; Who has taught us the way of holiness through the Mitzvot, and Who has inspired us to kindle the Festival Lights. Amen.

SANCTIFICATION OF THE DAY - KADESH

Leader: The Rabbis teach that in every generation we should allow ourselves to feel as if we personally came forth out of Egypt.

As believers in Yeshua, redeemed and delivered by His Blood, this Festival has special significance for us – as He was *our* Passover Lamb – and has delivered us from our Egypt ... our sinful life.

With grateful hearts let us give thanks to Adonai.

All: Baruch atah Adonai, eloheinu Melech ha-olam, she-heh-cheh-ya-nu, v'kee-ma-nu, v'hi-gee-ya-nu, laz-man ha-zeh.

Blessed are You O Lord our God, Ruler of the universe, who has kept us in life, sustained us and enabled us to reach this season and this Appointed Time. Amen.

Applying the Blood

THE FOUR CUPS

Leader: Four times during the course of the evening we partake of the wine. In Jewish Tradition, a full cup is symbolic of joy and thanksgiving. As we take each cup this evening, we call to mind one of the promises that Adonai made to our ancestors in Mitzaryim (Egypt), as He prepared them for their redemption. With each cup we remember a promise:

All: I will bring you out from under the yoke of the Egyptians; I will free you from being slaves; I will redeem you with an outstretched arm; I will take you as My own people and I will be your God.

THE FIRST CUP: Sanctification

I will bring you out from under the yoke of the Egyptians.

Leader: We take up the first cup and proclaim the holiness of this Day of Deliverance:

All: Baruch atah Adonai, Eloheinu Melech Ha-olam, borei pri ha-gafen.

Blessed are You O Lord our God, Ruler of the Universe, who creates the fruit of the vine. Amen.

WASHING OF HANDS: Urkhatz

Leader: Although it is traditional to wash one's hands before the Passover meal, during Yeshua's time, a servant would see to the need of each participant. However, it was during this portion of the Seder (often called Yeshua's Last Supper) where we see a humble act of our Messiah.

Scripture says: *He arose from the table, removed His outer garments and wrapped a towel around His waist. He then poured some water into a basin and began to wash the feet of His disciples and wipe them off with the towel, saying ... if I your Lord and Rabbi have washed your feet, you should also wash each other's feet. For I have given you an example, so that you shall do as I have done for you. (John 13:4, 5, 15)*

Yeshua acted as a servant and washed the feet of His disciples. Let us take to heart His example of servanthood and humility, as we offer the bowl of water and towel to one another, and share in this hand washing ceremony.

Leader: (Lifts the Bowl of Water)
All: Baruch atah Adonai, Eloheinu Melech ha-olam, asher kidshanu b'mitzo-tav, v'tzivanu, al n'teelas yadayim.

Blessed are you, O Lord our God, Ruler of the universe, who has taught us the way of holiness through the Mitzvot, and has commanded us to wash our hands.
(Humbly serve your neighbor with the bowl of water and towel)

REBIRTH AND RENEWAL: Karpas

Leader: *(Lifting the parsley and bowl of salt water)*

Passover is a holiday that comes in the springtime, when the earth is becoming green with life. The Karpas or parsley is a symbol of life and springtime. We dip it into salt water, which represents tears. This reminds us that life in Egypt was full of tears.
"...the people of Israel groaned under their bondage, and cried out for help,...and God heard their cry, and God remembered His covenant with Abraham, Isaac, and Jacob." (Ex 2:23,24)

All: Baruch atah Adonai Eloheinu Melech ha-olam borei pri hadamah.

Blessed are You, O Lord our God, Ruler of the universe, Who creates the fruit of the earth.

Leader: Now let's dip the Karpas in the salt water and eat it together.

THE FOUR QUESTIONS: Ma Nishtanah

Leader: Passover provides a yearly opportunity to teach our children Adonai's plan of redemption. It is commanded in the Torah to observe this service.

All: And when your children ask you, "What does this ceremony mean to you?" You will then tell them, "It is the Passover sacrifice to the LORD, Who passed over the houses of the Israelites in Egypt and spared our homes when He struck down the Egyptians." (Ex 12:25-27)

Leader: To make sure that the children fulfill this Scripture, there are four questions that a young child asks on Passover.

(A small child rises to ask the questions)

Ma nishtanah halaila hazeh mikol halelot! *(How different this night is from all the other nights!)*

Emondve -

WE ANSWER THE FOUR QUESTIONS OF THE PASSOVER

Leader: It is both a duty and a privilege to answer the four questions of Passover and to recite the mighty works of our faithful God. Let us answer these questions together.

First Child rises and asks: On all other nights, we eat either leavened bread or matzah. On this night why do we eat only matzah?

Leader: Adonai decreed that nothing with leaven would be eaten during the Passover season to remind us of the hasty departure from Egypt.

All: "With the dough brought from Egypt, they baked cakes of unleavened bread. The dough was without yeast because they had been driven out of Egypt and did not have time to prepare food..." (Ex 12:39)

All: Scripture also teaches that leaven symbolizes sin. Just as we cleanse our homes of leaven in order to celebrate the Passover, so we need to cleanse our lives of sin in order to enjoy all the blessings that come from Messiah Yeshua, our Passover Lamb.

Do you not know that a little leaven leavens the whole batch? Therefore purge out the old leaven, that you may be a new batch, since you truly are unleavened. For Yeshua, our Messiah has become our Passover Lamb.

During this season of Passover, let us break our old habits of sin and selfishness and begin a fresh, new and Holy life, set apart from the world.

Leader: *(Lift up Matzah Tosh)* Now comes one of the most interesting parts of the Seder for believers in Yeshua, the breaking of the middle Matzah.

Three matzot are placed in a special covering called the "Matzah Tosh". The Matzah Tosh is a three pocketed cover for the matzah, made of one single piece of cloth.

(Remove the middle Matzah from the Matzah Tosh and lift it up)

The middle Matzah is removed and broken. The larger piece is wrapped in a white cloth; it is called the Afikomenn meaning *"that which comes later"*.

Once wrapped, the Afikomenn is hidden as if it were buried, to be found and redeemed later for a reward. The smaller piece is saved and eaten before the meal. It is now time for each table to hide the Afikomenn, while the children cover their eyes.

Why are there three matzot? Some rabbis say it represents the HIGH PRIEST, LEVITES and PEOPLE of ISRAEL, or the three forms of worship in temple times. Some say it represents our Patriarchs Abraham, Isaac and Jacob. But the question must be asked: why is the middle matzah broken, wrapped and hidden? So why is the middle matzah broken, hidden and brought back!

This tradition, which has been celebrated for thousands of years, is a beautiful picture of the Father, Son and Holy Spirit. Remember the Matzah Tosh made of one piece of cloth that contains three pieces of matzah. We now can see the picture of three in one; for us who believe in Yeshua, it is no mystery. The Son left heaven, was offered up, buried, and brought back; ransoms for all that believe in Him.

(Raise the remaining piece of matzah)

All: This is the bread of affliction which our forefathers ate in the land of Egypt. All who are hungry - let them come and eat. All who are needy - let them come and celebrate the Passover with us.

Leader: Baruch atah Adonai Eloheinu Melech ha-olam, asher kidshanu b'mitzvo-tav, v'tzivanu, al achilat matzah.

All: Blessed are you O Lord our God, Ruler of the universe, who has taught us Your ways through the Commandments and has commanded us to eat unleavened bread.

Leader: Let us now share a piece of this unleavened bread of Passover. (Distribute the other half among the people at the table)

Second Small Child rises and asks: On all other nights we eat all kinds of vegetables. On this night why do we eat only bitter herbs?

Leader: Bitter herbs are eaten to remind us of the bitterness the Egyptians caused in the lives of the children of Israel.

All: "The Egyptians came to dread the Israelites and worked them ruthlessly. They made their lives bitter with hard labor in brick and mortar and with all kinds of work in the fields." (Ex 1:12-14)

Leader: As we dip some maror, which is represented by the horseradish, onto a piece of Matzah, let us allow the bitter taste to cause us to shed tears of compassion for the sorrow that the Israelites knew thousands of years ago.

Leader: Baruch atah Adonai Eloheinu Melech ha-olam, asher kidshanu b'mitzvo-tav, v'tzivanu, al achilat maror.

All: Blessed are You, O Lord our God, Ruler of the universe, who has taught us your ways through the Commandments and has commanded us to eat bitter herbs. (All eat of the maror)

Third Small Child rises and asks: On all other nights we do not dip our vegetables even once. On this night why do we dip them twice?

Leader: The kharoset, a mixture of apples, dates and nuts, represents the mud that was mixed with straw to make the bricks to build Pharaoh's cities.

We have eaten the dry matzah and the bitter herbs as commanded; now we eat the Kharoset to remind us that in Yeshua there can still be sweetness, even in the midst of the bitterest circumstances.

Now each of us will take a bit of the maror, the bitter herb, and dip it into the kharoset; thus, we dip our food twice. (All eat)
Leader: Our tradition today is to once again take matzah, this time two pieces, and make a sandwich with the horseradish and kharoset (all eat)

Another sandwich was eaten with Lamb during temple times in Jerusalem. With the matzah and lamb, dipped in maror Yeshua spoke of his betrayal:

All: *"I say to you, that one of you will betray Me." The disciples began looking at one another, at a loss to know of which one He was speaking. There was reclining on Jesus' bosom one of His disciples, whom Jesus loved. So Simon Peter gestured to him, and said to him, "Tell us who it is of whom He is speaking." He, leaning back thus on Jesus' bosom, said to Him, "Lord, who is it?"*

Jesus then answered, "That is the one for whom I shall dip the morsel and give it to him." So when He had dipped the morsel, He took and gave it to Judas, the son of Simon Iscariot. (John 13:21-26)

Forth small child rises and asks: On all other nights we eat our meals sitting or reclining. On this night, why do we eat only reclining?

Leader: While still awaiting release from Pharaoh, Adonai instructed the Israelites to eat the Passover in haste, their loins girded, their staffs in their hands, and their sandals upon their feet. In ancient times, the posture of reclining at meals was a sign of a free man. Today in freedom we all may recline and freely enjoy the Passover Seder.

Leader: Yeshua said: *"I tell you the truth, everyone who sins is a slave to sin. Now a slave has no permanent place in the family, but a son belongs to it forever. So if the Son sets you free, you are free indeed"* (John 8:34-36).

Leader: How much more, having been brought out of darkness into Yeshua's light, can we truly say…

All: Once we were slaves, but now we are free!

TELLING THE PASSOVER STORY

MAGGID

(A Responsive Reading)

Leader: Now let us recount the story of Passover to one another.

Reader 1: The Bible teaches that during a great famine in the land of Canaan, the sons of Israel journeyed to Egypt to purchase food. There they were reunited with their brother Joseph. Because of his influence, they were permitted to dwell in the fertile plains of Goshen. At first, the House of Israel numbered less than 80 souls. But in time, their numbers swelled, their flocks increased, and they became a mighty people.

ALL: And then there arose a new Pharaoh, one who did not know Joseph. He beheld the might of Israel, and he feared that in time of war, the sons of Jacob might join themselves with Egypt's foes.

READER 2: And so he subdued the Israelites, and he afflicted them with cruel labor. Task masters were placed over the Israelites, to compel them to make bricks and to build Pharaoh's great storage cities of Ramses and Pithom.

ALL: But despite their hardship, they continued to thrive, just as God had promised. This caused Pharaoh even greater alarm, and he ordered the slaughter of Israel's infant sons. By his command, every male child born to the Hebrews was to be cast into the Nile and drowned.

READER 3: How sober were the afflictions of the Jewish people. In anguish, we cried to the God of our Fathers. And God heard our cry. God remembered His covenant. And God raised up a deliverer, a redeemer, the man Moses. And He sent Moses to Pharaoh's court to declare the *commandment of the Lord...*

ALL: Let my people go.

READER 4: But Pharaoh would not hearken to the Lord of Hosts. And so, Moses pronounced God's judgment on Pharaoh's house and on Pharaoh's land. Plagues were poured out upon the Egyptians, upon their crops, and upon their flocks.

ALL: But Pharaoh's heart was hardened. He would not yield to the will of God. He would not let the House of Jacob depart.

The Second Cup - Plagues
I will free you from being slaves

Leader: Adonai heard the groaning of His people and sent Moses to the rescue. He warned Moses that the message would not be well received and that additional persuasion would be necessary.

All: *But I know that the king of Egypt will not let you go unless a mighty hand compels him. So I will stretch out my hand and strike the Egyptians with all the wonders that I will perform among them. After that, he will let you go! (Ex 3:18-20)*

Leader: *In our tradition,* a full cup is the symbol of joy. Though we celebrate Adonai's deliverance, our happiness cannot be complete knowing others had to die for our redemption from slavery in Egypt, in the same manner that our Messiah Yeshua had to die for our redemption from sin.

We shall therefore diminish the wine in our cups as we recall the plagues visited upon the Egyptians. As we repeat each plague three times, let us dip a finger into the cup, allowing a drop of wine to fall, reducing the fullness of our cup of joy.

All:

Blood
Frogs
Lice
Swarms
Blight
Boils
Hail
Locusts
Darkness
Death of the Firstborn

(We do not yet drink of the second cup)

Leader: With sadness we remember those that perished in the plagues in Egypt. It is also with sadness that at this time in our Seder, we stand in silence as we take time now to remember those who perished in the holocaust of Europe.

The Passover Lamb: Zeroah

Leader: In the words of Rabbi Gamaliel, the grandson of Rabbi Hillel, and some say the grandfather of the Apostle Paul, "There are three symbols that are so important and so meaningful that no Seder is complete unless they are fully explained". These symbols are the Passover Lamb, the matzah, and the maror. We have experienced two of these symbols, the matzah (unleavened bread) and the maror (bitter herbs).

Leader: *(Lifting the shank bone)* Since the destruction of the second Temple, lamb is not served at the Passover Seder. This roasted shank bone remains, being symbolic of the Passover lamb.

The blood of a lamb on the doorpost marked the houses of the children of Israel, signifying their obedience to Adonai's command.

All: *"That same night they are to eat the meat roasted over the fire, along with bitter herbs, and bread made without yeast. This is how you are to eat it: with your cloak tucked into your belt, your sandals on your feet and your staff in your hand. Eat it in haste; it is the LORD's Passover. On that same night I will pass through Egypt and strike down every firstborn--both men and animals--and I will bring judgment on all the gods of Egypt. I am the LORD. The blood will be a sign for you on the houses where you are; and when I see the blood, I will pass over you. No destructive plague will touch you when I strike Egypt" (Ex 12:8, 12-13)*

Leader: Adonai was very specific about what kind of lamb would qualify. The family brought it into the home before Passover for inspection and observation. The lamb had to be a perfect male, without any spot or blemish. No bone of the lamb was to be broken.

The Passover lamb was, and still is, a beautiful symbol of the coming Messiah. Yeshua was the perfect sacrifice, sinless and blameless in the sight of Adonai. He was scrutinized by Israel during His public ministry, and He was found without fault or blemish. In spite of His torturous death, not one of His bones was broken.

Leader: We are reminded by Moses that it was the Lord Himself who redeemed the children of Israel from slavery.

All: *So the Lord brought us out of Egypt with a mighty hand and an outstretched arm, with great* *terror and with miraculous signs and wonders. (Deut 26:8)*

Leader: On that same night I will pass through Egypt.

All: I, and not an angel.

Leader: And strike down every first born – of both men and animals.

All: I, and not a seraph.

Leader: And I will bring judgment on all the gods of Egypt.

All: I, and not a messenger.

Leader: I am the Lord (Ex 12:12)

All: I myself, and none other.

Roasted Egg - Beitzah

Leader: The last item on the Seder Plate, the egg, like the shank bone only symbolizes a sacrifice. The egg represents the chagigah sacrifices that were offered at the Temple in Jerusalem during the holidays. It is regarded as a symbol of mourning since the Temple was destroyed in 70 AD. But for the Messianic Believer Yeshua HaMashiach is the final and sufficient sacrifice.

All: But when Yeshua had offered for all time, a single sacrifice for sins, He sat down at the right hand of Adonai. (Heb 10:11)

Dayenu - It Would Have Been Sufficient

Leader: How many are the gifts Adonai our God has bestowed upon us!

If the Lord had merely rescued us, but had not judged the Egyptians; *All:* Dayenu

If He had only destroyed their gods, but had not parted the Sea of Reeds; *All:* Dayenu

If He had only drowned our enemies, but had not fed us with manna; *All:* Dayenu

If He had only led us through the desert, but had not given us the Shabbat; **All:** Dayenu

If He had only given us the Torah, but not the land of Israel; **All:** Dayenu

(Let Us All Sing together)

Dayenu

Ilu hotsi hotsianu, hotsianu mi-Mitzrayim,
        hotisanu mi-Mitzrayim, Dayenu.

Ilu natan natan lanu, natan lanu et ha-Shabot,
        natan lanu et ha-Shabot, Dayenu

Ilu natan natan lanu, natan lanu et ha-Torah,
        natan lanu et ha-Torah, Dayenu.

Ilu natan natan lanu, natan lanu et Y'shua,
        natan lanu et Yeshua. Dayenu

Leader: But the Holy one, Blessed be He, provided all of these Blessings for our ancestors. And not only these, but so many more.

(Let us drink the second cup)

The Meal is Served - Shulchan Oreich

Leader: Exodus 12:14 commands us:

All: "Now this day will be a memorial to you, and you shall celebrate it as a feast to the LORD; throughout your generations you are to celebrate it as a permanent ordinance".

Leader: It is good to read and obey the Words of our God.

All: Blessed are You, O Lord, for You have, in mercy, supplied all our needs. You have given us Messiah Yeshua, forgiveness for sin, life abundant and life everlasting. Hallelujah!!!

Leader: It is time now to eat our meal. Let us enjoy our meal and our fellowship, and let us thank our God for His Blessings.

All: Blessed are You, O Lord our God, who creates all kinds of foods. May our meal and fellowship be Blessed with your presence. Amen.

(After the dinner, all items except the elements of Passover are removed from the table)

SEARCH FOR THE AFIKOMENN

Leader: It is now time for the children to search for the Afikomenn, and redeem it for a reward. So children, start looking and when you find it, take it to your table leader who will give you a reward.

(Once the Afikomenn has been redeemed)

Leader: It is time for us to share the Afikomenn, the final food eaten at the Passover. It is shared as the Passover Lamb was shared from the time of the Exodus until the destruction of the Temple in 70 AD. We are instructed that the Afikomen should linger in our mouths.

Yeshua pronounced the traditional Blessing:

Leader: Baruch atah Adonai Eloheinu Melech ha-olam, asher kidshanu b'mitzvo-tav, v'tzivanu, al achilat matzah.

All: Blessed are You, O Lord our God, Ruler of the universe, Who has taught us the way of holiness through the Mitzvot, and has commanded us to eat unleavened bread.

Leader: It was at this point that Yeshua changed a few of the words of the Passover; as He took the matzah after offering the Blessing, He then said: *"Take this each of you and eat of it, and when you do let it remind you of My body which will be given up for you* When you eat the Passover, do it in remembrance of Me".

Leader: These were strange words that had never been said at the Passover, before. "What did He mean, His body would be given up for us", was most likely in the minds of those who were with Him". It is clear to us now: He was *our* Passover Lamb, whose body was given as an offering for our Redemption.

Leader: Let us now eat the matzah, remembering the body of the Lamb of God that was freely given for you and me, as payment for our sins. Allow the taste to linger in your mouth as you meditate on this work that provided the only way to save our souls.

THE THIRD CUP - REDEMPTION

I will redeem you with an outstretched arm

Leader: In the same manner, Yeshua took the cup; it was the third cup of the evening, and after He said the traditional Blessing over the cup, He again startled those in attendance when He said *"take this cup, each of you, and when you drink of it let it remind you of the blood that will be spilled for you"*. Broken body, spilled blood? What on earth is he talking about…. this is getting frightening - may have been the thoughts that now completely filled the minds of the Disciples. Never before had they heard such words at a Seder – broken matzah yes, blood of the Passover lamb yes, but never in such context.

As believers, we now know that Yeshua was giving a picture of what was to come, and *what had been told through the Prophets*. The picture is now complete … the Lamb of God had been offered up for our sins and sealed by the blood of that same Lamb. He was and is, our Passover Lamb.

Leader: Baruch atah Adonai Eloheinu Melech ha-olam, borei pri ha-gafen.

All: Blessed art You, O Lord our God, Ruler of the universe, Who creates the fruit of the vine.

THE PROPHET ELIJAH

Leader: To see if Elijah has come to our Seder, we will send a child to look outside and call his name.

(A child goes to an outside door and calls for Elijah)

Leader: According to legend Elijah visits every Jewish home at the Seder and sips the cup. At our Seder, the cup of Elijah is filled but not drunk, as it remains on the table as a sign of Adonai's further Messianic promise:

All: See, I will send you the prophet Elijah before that great and dreadful day of the Lord comes. He will turn the hearts of the fathers to their children and the hearts of the children to their fathers. *(Mal 4:4-6)*

Leader: Before the birth of John the Baptizer, an angel of the Lord said:

All: And he will go on before the Lord in the spirit and power of Elijah, to make ready a people prepared for the Lord. *(Luke 1:17)*

Leader: Later Yeshua spoke of John:

All: And if you are willing to accept it, he is the Elijah who was to come. (Matt 11:14

Leader: It was the same John who when he first saw Yeshua coming down to the river, said:

All: Look, the Lamb of God, Who takes away the sin of the world (John 1:29)

All: And they asked him, "Why do the teachers of the law say that Elijah must come first?" Yeshua replied, "To be sure, Elijah does come first, and restores all things. Why then is it written that the Son of Man must suffer much and be rejected? But I tell you, Elijah has come, and they have done to him everything they wished, just as it is written about him". (Mark 9:11-13)

For all the Prophets and the Law prophesied until John. And if you are willing to accept it, he is the Elijah who was to come. He, who has ears, let him hear". (Matt 11:13-15)

LET US SING ELIYAHU

Eliyahu ha-Navi

Eliyahu ha-Navi, Eliyahu ha-Tishbi,
Eliyahu, Eliyahu, Eliyahu ha-Giladi.
Bimheirah, b'yameinu yavo eileinu,
Im Ma-shiach ben David, im Ma-shiach ben David.
Eliyah ha-Navi, Eliyahu ha-Tishbi,
Eliyahu, Eliyahu, Eliyahu ha-Giladi.

THE FOURTH CUP - PRAISE

I will take you as My own people and I will be your God.

Leader: And Scripture says that when they had finished the Passover Seder, they sang songs and hymns. The tradition was to take the cup for the last time of the evening, the cup of praise. Yet in our joy of the evening, we don't want to miss one more thing that Yeshua said to His Disciples and to us:

All: "But I say to you, I will not drink of this fruit of the vine from now on until that day when I drink *it new with you in My Father's kingdom." (Matt 26:9)*

Leader: We can drink of the cup of praise this evening, but won't it be wonderful to drink the cup of praise with Messiah Yeshua as He promised?

Let us raise our cups one more time and give thanks for the great promise of Adonai:

All: I will take you as my own people and I will be your God. (Ex 6:7)

Leader: Yeshua probably sang this or other of the Hallel Psalms in the upper room with His disciples. Only hours before His arrest and eventual crucifixion, He sang of love, joy, and confidence in Adonai. He willingly became our Passover Lamb, paying the price to redeem us. Let us rejoice together in the Hallel, giving praise to Him Who hears and acts on our behalf.

All: Give thanks to Adonai, who is good, His love endures forever!
Give thanks to the God of gods, His love endures forever!
Give thanks to the Lord of lords, His love endures forever!
Who alone works great wonders, His love endures forever!
Who, with understanding, made the heavens, His love endures forever!
Who stretched out the earth above the waters, His love endures forever!
Who made the great lights, His love endures forever!
The sun, to rule by day, His love endures forever!
The moon and stars, to rule by night, His love endures forever!
To him Who struck down the firstborn of Egypt, His love endures forever!
And brought Israel out from among them, His love endures forever!
With a mighty hand and outstretched arm, His love endures forever!
To Him who divided the Sea of Reeds asunder, His love endures forever!
And brought Israel through the midst of it, His love endures forever!
But swept Pharaoh and his army into the Sea of Reeds, His love endures forever!

To Him who led his people through the desert, His love endures forever!
Give thanks to the God of heaven, His love endures forever! Ps 136:1-16, 26)

Conclusion

Leader: Our Seder now has ended; let us conclude with the traditional wish that we will celebrate Passover next year in Jerusalem.

L'shanah haba'ah bi Yerushalayim

L'shanah haba'ah bi Yerushalayim

L'shanah haba'ah bi Yerushalayim

L'shanah haba'ah bi Yerushalayim

Next year in Jerusalem!